Decimals on a Diamond

by Kathleen Fitz
illustrated by Suzanne Mogensen

HOUGHTON MIFFLIN   BOSTON

Printed in China

ISBN 10: 0-618-90000-4
ISBN 13: 978-0-618-90000-8

789 0940 16 15 14 13

4500411355

Crack! The ball sailed into the air and landed in right field. Mai ran past first base and then second base. She headed for third and saw the coach waving at her to go all the way. As her foot hit home base, she heard the umpire yell, "Safe!"

Mai took off her batting helmet and sat beside Matthew on the bench. "Excellent!" he exclaimed. "This brings your batting average up to .545."

"Where did that number come from?" Mai asked.

"A batting average is a decimal. The decimal shows the percent of hits for your total number of times at bat. You've been up to bat 33 times this season and you have had 18 hits. Eighteen is a part of the whole of 33. I divided 18 by 33 and got .545. Look at this. I figured the batting averages of everyone on the team."

Name	Batting Average
Omar	.331
Helene	.152
Anita	.411
Yuri	.219
Diego	.421
Julio	.309
Hannah	.198
Nada	.317
Adam	.502
Darius	.498
Matthew	.095
Mai	.545

"So the higher the number, the better your batting average?" Mai asked.

"Exactly," Matthew said. "My number is low because I'm not a very good batter."

"Well, you are the best at math!" Mai smiled. "How can I tell which number is highest?"

Matthew explained, "First, we look at the tenths place. The highest number in the tenths place is 5. Two players have batting averages with 5 in the tenths place. Then we compare the hundredths places to find which number is highest."

Read·Think·Write Who has the highest batting average?

"I see," said Mai. "Wow, I have the highest batting average!"

"Yes," said Matthew. "You've gotten more hits for all the times you batted than anyone else."

"What's that paper?" asked Yuri. Matthew showed him the chart. "That's like what they do for the major league players!" Yuri exclaimed.

Soon all of the players were interested. Even the coach wanted to see what Matthew had done. The team asked Matthew to rank the players based on their batting averages. Matthew took the chart home and put all the numbers in order. He made a chart ranking the players by batting average.

Name	Batting Average
Mai	.545
Adam	.502
Darius	.498
Diego	.421
Anita	.411
Omar	.331
Nada	.317
Julio	.309
Yuri	.219
Hannah	.198
Helene	.152
Matthew	.095

The next day, Omar had a sheet of the games each team in the league had won and lost.

Team	Games Won	Games Lost
Hawks	6	3
Tigers	4	4
Lions	1	6
Bears	5	4
Eagles	4	4
Wolves	6	1

Omar pointed out that the Hawks had won six out of nine games. The Wolves had won six out of seven games. Which team was in first place?

Matthew explained, "You have to divide the number of games won by the total number of games played." Matthew and Omar completed the chart.

Team	Games Won	Games Lost	Total Games Played	Win/Loss Percent
Hawks	6	3	9	.67
Tigers	4	4	8	.50
Lions	1	6	7	.16
Bears	5	4	9	.56
Eagles	4	4	8	.50
Wolves	6	1	7	.86

Read·Think·Write Which team has the highest win/loss percent?

Omar made a new chart. He used the win/loss percents to put the teams in order from first to last.

Team	Win/Loss Percent
Wolves	.86
Hawks	.67
Bears	.56
Eagles	.50
Tigers	.50
Lions	.16

"Oh, no!" cried Anita. "We're in second place!"

"The Eagles and Tigers are tied," said Mai.

The coach explained that the chart might change after all the teams played nine games. That week the Wolves played the Lions, and the Lions won. Then the Tigers played the Wolves. The Wolves won. Finally, the Eagles played the Lions, and the Eagles won. Matthew made another chart.

Team	Games Won	Games Lost	Total Games Played	Win/Loss Percent
Hawks	6	3	9	.67
Tigers	4	5	9	.44
Lions	2	7	9	.22
Bears	5	4	9	.56
Eagles	5	4	9	.56
Wolves	7	2	9	.78

"How do you rank the teams?" asked Anita.

Mai explained, "Put the decimals in order."

"I use a number line to help me," added Omar.

"A place-value chart is another way," explained Matthew. "Start by comparing numbers in the tenths place. Then look at the hundredths place."

Mai said, "We've got work to do."

All the Hawk players put their hands in the middle of a circle and cheered, "Go Hawks!"

Read·Think·Write Now that all the teams have played nine games, which team is in first place? Which two teams are tied?

1. Draw a place-value chart showing ones, tenths, hundredths, and thousandths. Write the batting average .361 in the place-value chart.

2. Draw a number line. Circle the following win/loss percents on the number line.

   0.46   0.59   0.41   0.52

3. In Question 2, which circled number on the number line is the greatest win/loss percent?

4. Understand Sequence Order the following win/loss percents from greatest to least.

   0.83   0.38   0.32   0.70   0.67

Activity

With a partner, write the following decimals on place-value charts.

0.52   0.39   0.729   0.402

Next, write the numbers on a number line.

Finally, write the numbers in order from least to greatest.